EARTH'S BIOMES

CHAPARRAL AND SCRUB

EARTH'S BIOMES

CHAPARRAL AND SCRUB

TOM WARHOL

Marshall Cavendish
Benchmark
New York

To Lisa, for everything.

Marshall Cavendish Benchmark
99 White Plains Road
Tarrytown, New York 10591-9001
www.marshallcavendish.us

Text and maps copyright © 2007 by Marshall Cavendish Corporation
Map by Robert Romagnoli

All Web sites were available and accurate when this book was sent to press

Editor: Karen Ang
Editorial Director: Michelle Bisson
Art Director: Anahid Hamparian
Series Designer: Patrice Sheridan

Library of Congress Cataloging-in-Publication Data

Warhol, Tom.
Chaparral and scrub / by Tom Warhol.
p. cm.—(Earth's biomes)
Summary: "Explores chaparral and scrub biomes and covers where they are
located, as well as the plants and animals that inhabit them"—
Provided by publisher.
Includes bibliographical references and index.
ISBN-13: 978-0-7614-2195-5
ISBN-10: 0-7614-2195-5
1. Shrubland ecology—Juvenile literature. 2. Mediterranean-type
ecosystems—Juvenile literature. I. Title. II. Series.

QH541.5.S55.W37 2006
577.3'8—dc22
2006015824

Front cover: Renosterveld in South Africa
Title page: Mediterranean scrub
Back cover: Scrub in Chile

Photo research by Candlepants, Inc.

The photographs in this book are used by permission and through the courtesy of: *Tom Warhol:* 7, 22, 50, 13. *Photo Researchers Inc.:* Dennis Flaherty, 8; Dan Suzio, 18; Mark Boulton, 21; Laurie Campbell, 24; Georg Gerster, 32; Mark Boutlon, 37; Kenneth W. Fink, 39; B.G. Thomson, 43; Peter Bowater, 64; Geoff Bryant, 65; Nuridsany et Perrenou, 66; Tom McHugh, 68. *Minden Pictures:* Norbert Wu, 15; Philip Friskorn/Fotonatura, 31; Greg Harold/Auscape, 42; Gerry Ellis, 46. *Peter Arnold Inc.:* Jean Roche, 3, 63; Walter H. Hodge, 17, 48; David McNew, 26; Martin Harvey, 34; Tom Vezo, 52; J.J. Alcalay, 57, 71; Gunter Ziesler, 58. *Corbis:* Rick D'Elia, 28; Jon Hicks, 40; Len Robinson; Frank Lane Picture Agency, 44; Wolfgang Kaehler, 56, back cover; Andrew Brown /Ecoscene, 60.
Printed in China
3 5 6 4 2

CONTENTS

INTRODUCTION

MALLEE, FYNBOS, AND MAQUIS

The smell of sage drifts along on the hot, dry winds that blow across the foothills and up into the mountains of the Coast Range in southern California. Thunderclouds drift eastward from the Pacific Ocean, offering hope of a cooling shower to this parched landscape. A loud *boom* punctuates the moaning of the wind. A flash of lightning signals that this storm will not bring much-needed rain but the exact opposite—fire. The lightning easily ignites the dry, densely growing shrubs, and the oils in the evergreen leaves add fuel to the fire that now erupts, moving swiftly uphill through the packed growth.

Such a hot and intense fire quickly lays waste to everything in its path, scattering animals, birds, and reptiles ahead of the flames. Seeing this devastation would make one wonder whether anything could grow in this area again. This is the beauty and resilience of the chaparral. Chaparral is the North American formation of the mediterranean scrub biome. Not only do many plant species survive fires, but they are actually dependent on the fire so they can spread and grow.

California's coastal sage scrub communities are one of the rarest plant communities in North America. Their location along the slopes above the Pacific make them prime targets for residential development.

By the following winter, green growth appears atop the ash-covered soil. Wildflowers soon bloom, offering their spectacular displays of color to the recently barren landscape. The flowers grow so swiftly and so strongly, almost like they know that their time is short. Deer and other herbivores feed on the fresh green leaves. When the second year after the fire comes, the chaparral shrubs begin sending out new branches and leaves. By the third and fourth growing seasons, they crowd out the wildflowers, and by the sixth season, their tangle is practically impenetrable again.

Mediterranean scrub grows mainly on western coasts of continents, as here in California, or in a ring around the Mediterranean Sea.

1

WHAT IS MEDITERRANEAN SCRUB?

Densely growing shrubs, sometimes with scattered trees growing above and herbs and grasses beneath, is the common form of mediterranean scrub—also known as mediterranean shrublands—all around the world. Most scrub plants typically have small, stiff, thick leaves called sclerophylls. These plants are evergreen, meaning they don't shed their leaves during a cold or dry period without first replacing them. (The types of plants that do shed their leaves each year without replacement are called deciduous.)

Mediterranean scrub occurs almost exclusively between 30 degrees and 45 degrees latitude, north and south, on the western coasts of continents, facing cold, drying offshore winds. Scrub habitats are also found along the foothills around the Mediterranean Sea.

These shrublands form in particular climates, know as mediterranean climates—hot, dry summers and cool, wet winters. The shrublands typically grow in poor soils on steep slopes where other vegetation has a hard time taking hold. Most mediterranean shrublands are subject to regular fires, both natural and human-caused.

Because of the specific conditions necessary for its growth, mediterranean scrub is found in only five locations throughout the world, and covers only 1 percent of Earth's land, which is less than any other biome. Each of these formations of scrub, while similar in appearance, has very different animal and plant species, kinds of soil, and levels of rainfall and groundwater. They often grow in a mosaic with other habitats, such as oak woodland, grassland, or other shrub formations.

The largest expression of this biome is in the Mediterranean Basin, which is along the ring of land surrounding the Mediterranean Sea. Regionally, it's known as matorral, but each country has their own name for the different formations.

Renosterveld is the South African formation and is the most biologically rich and unique of the scrub habitats.

Scrub Habitats of the World

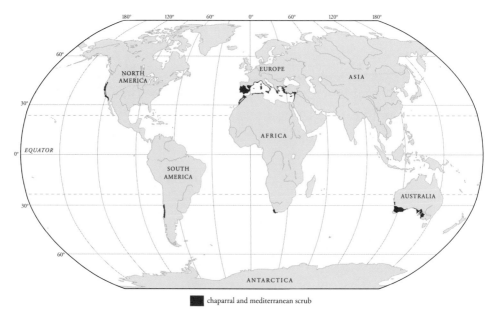

chaparral and mediterranean scrub

Australia's shrublands, known as mallee scrub, grow along the southern coast of this island continent. The dominant plants in the two distinct areas that make up this formation are scrub forms of eucalyptus, normally a tree species.

Each of the American continents has its own version of the mediterranean scrub biome. California, on the west coast of the United States, may have the largest continuous formation of mediterranean scrub. Chaparral and coastal sage occur along the western flanks of the Coast Ranges and the Sierra Nevada Range. Similarly, in central Chile in South America, the lower slopes of the two parallel mountain ranges, the Cordillera de la Costa and the Andes Mountains, support two forms, matorral and jaral.

EVOLUTION OF SCRUB FORMATIONS

Mediterranean scrub may be one of the youngest biomes on the planet. Many of the areas now occupied by scrub were once forested, when conditions were wetter in the time between glacial periods. The reason that the scrub habitats formed is due to the evolution of the mediterranean climate as much as any other factor.

Ice Ages of geological history have been a time of movement back and forth between glacial periods, when ice sheets covered significant parts of Earth, and interglacial periods, like now, when Earth has warmed and the glaciers melted, or retreated, back toward the poles. As the ice sheets moved back and forth across the landscape, climates changed and so did the vegetation and animal life living in these areas.

After the glaciers last receded around the Mediterranean Basin, forests colonized the higher elevations and grassland dominated on the lower slopes and in the valleys. At this time, the climate was moister and cooler than it is now. Gradually, forests invaded the grasslands, but they were not made up of the same species that were found in the higher elevations. Oaks and pines were more successful in the Mediterranean Basin region.

Paleobotanists—scientists who study ancient plants—have found evidence that the chaparral of central California did not appear until about three to five million years ago. They think that the shrubs that now dominate the chaparral communities originally began as plants growing in the understory of forests.

As the climate gradually warmed up and became drier in all of the mediterranean regions, the plants that we know of as scrub plants adapted and were able to survive. Some of them became very tolerant of the dry conditions by evolving more extensive root systems, while other plants took on a habit of dormancy that helped them avoid the worst of the dry season.

The plants that make up the five mediterranean shrubland formations reflect the variety of sources that they evolved from. At the end of the Paleozoic era, about 250 million years ago, the continents were all attached as one supercontinent called Pangaea. Species of plants and animals were able to spread and move freely across the continent in response to climate change without oceans as barriers to their movement.

As the tectonic plates—continent-sized pieces of Earth's crust—shifted, the continents separated, and the plants and animals were isolated on their respective continents. Some continents remained connected for a while, such as the southern continents Australia, Antarctica, and South America, allowing continued exchange of species. Other continents become connected later on—such as North America and South America—fostering a new exchange and mix of species.

As a result, the mediterranean regions support a variety of species that existed there before they acquired a mediterranean climate, as well as another group that evolved along with the climate.

Plants grow right up to the edges of the bluffs along the Pacific Ocean in coastal sage scrub communities.

Each of the five regions has become what it is today due to varied influences. Some have changed, because of new environmental conditions or human influence, from a more complex ecosystem, like a forest, to a less complex one, like the shrublands. Others are at an early stage of recovery after having endured long periods of use by humans. Then there are those that have reached what ecologists call a climax and are maintaining themselves in the same form, until some kind of major disturbance—fire, climate change, land clearing—comes along.

In some regions, such as Chile, southern Europe, and Morocco, scrub habitats may have formed due to human settlement and alteration of the landscape. Because of widespread clearing of these woodlands for farms, pastures, firewood, and other purposes, a new type of vegetation took hold, maintained by periodic human-set fires and grazing by domestic cattle.

ADAPTATION

Because the mediterranean shrublands are so separate from each other and so different from their surrounding environments, some of the plant and animal species there have evolved specifically to suit the individual formations and live nowhere else.

The science of where plants and animals live is called biogeography. Ecologists study how species of various organisms become adapted to their different habitats. One large population of a particular species may become broken up into smaller populations because of some environmental change—a river's course alters and divides a habitat, or a change in climate strands part of a population on a mountaintop.

Over time, that species adapts specifically to the new conditions, even to the point of becoming a whole new species. Many scrub plants have taken on their current form because of environmental factors— fire, soils, climate—but were probably part of a similar but differently

In California, monarch butterflies spend the winter in Monterey Pine and eucalyptus groves.

adapted species in the past. There are more than six hundred species of eucalyptus, trees and shrubs of Australia with fragrant and flammable oils in their leaves. Each of these has adapted to specific conditions in their environment—minor or major changes in soil, moisture, or microclimate.

When a plant or animal adapts to a unique environment, requiring specifically what that environment provides, that species is said to be endemic to that particular ecosystem. The geometric tortoise lives only in the renosterveld of South Africa. It has become adapted to that habitat, feeding only on the plants that grow there. These preferences have placed this tortoise species on the endangered list, since its habitat is rapidly being destroyed.

Convergence, or parallel evolution, occurs when different organisms take on a similar appearance and/or behaviors because they have adapted to similar habitats in very different parts of the world. There are very few native species of plants or animals that live in more than one mediterranean shrubland habitat, but many of them share similar shapes, physiology, or behaviors. Most shrubs and trees in scrub formations have developed sclerophyllous leaves. This may be an adaptation that evolved independently in the different fire-prone scrub habitats.

California lilac is a common plant of California's chaparral communities, covering the hillside in a purple "mist" when the flowers open in spring.

2

SCRUB BASICS

Although the five mediterranean scrub formations all share common characteristics that enable them to be grouped within the same biome, the most striking thing among them is their variation. They are all remarkably diverse for such dry habitats. Grouped together, all five formations contain roughly 20 percent of the world's plant species.

CLIMATE

One of the main reasons that scrub habitats have evolved as they have is the climate where they occur, between moist and arid lands. A set of unique conditions has helped to create the mediterranean climate.

As trade winds move toward the poles during the summer, they carry very little moisture with them and, consequently, they dry out the landscape. Many days can pass in mediterranean regions during the summer when there will be hardly a cloud in the sky. This near constant sunlight and the high temperatures make for a very harsh environment.

Intense drying foehn (pronounced "fahn,") winds make conditions even more extreme in some of the formations. These winds carry super-heated air that builds up over interior deserts. In North America, the Sonoran Desert is the source for the Santa Ana winds, while in the Mediterranean Basin, the Sahara Desert provides fuel for the foehn winds that wilt crops in the eastern part of the basin. This is a case where the conditions created by one biome (deserts) affects the conditions in another (mediterranean scrub).

Most regions of Earth either have rainy seasons during the summer and a drier period in the winter months, or rain occurs year-round. Mediterranean shrublands receive most of their rain during the winter, when the temperatures are mild and westerly winds carry moisture over these regions on their way toward the equator. So, the best times for scrub plants to grow are during the winter and spring months.

This much-needed rain is vital to these regions, but still only amounts to about 11 to 35 inches (275 to 900 millimeters) a year. Compare this to tropical forests, where between 13 and 26 *feet*

Chaparral often mixes with small woodland trees and is interspersed with agricultural or pasture lands in California.

(4 to 8 meters) of rain fall each year. Rain falls in every month of the year in rainforests as well, while scrub habitats receive rain only during their winter or rainy season, four or five months out of the year. Plants in chaparral and other scrub formations take what moisture they can get, though, using it to maintain themselves throughout the dry season.

Some regions, like Chile and California, may not get a lot of rain, but they do get other forms of moisture. Fog frequently forms over the oceans and moves over land, creating very high humidity. Plants and animals are able to absorb this moisture.

Summer rains do occur in some regions, and they can be significant in Australia and South Africa.

GEOLOGY AND SOILS

The landscape of mediterranean regions tends to be very uneven, with steep valleys and sharp peaks. This is how the mosaic of varied habitat types forms, as each of these pockets can have their own microclimate, soil type, and plant species.

The soils of mediterranean regions are as varied as the topography, ranging from mineral-poor soils formed from very old rocks in South Africa and Australia to soils formed from more recent erosion of limestone or other sedimentary rocks in the Americas.

The dry conditions in some of these regions make the process of decay, in which weather and organisms break down plant matter, much slower. The build-up of dry, flammable leaves serves as ideal fuel to carry very hot fires through the landscape.

Mediterranean scrub vegetation, especially chaparral, grows on very steep slopes made up of loose, rocky soils. Without these plants holding the soil in place with their root systems, the ground can become very unstable. Landslides can occur in areas where fires are followed by heavy rains. With no vegetation to deflect the rain water, the soils quickly become saturated and slide downhill, clogging streams and even causing houses and other buildings to collapse. Since scrub plants are some of the only plants able to grow on these soils, they are responsible for keeping them stable and preventing landslides.

Of the five regions of mediterranean scrub, three are along active fault lines, meaning that earthquakes and volcanoes can occur there on a regular basis. The rocks are very young and mountains are still actively being created by these processes. An earthquake occurs when tectonic plates collide, one forced underneath the other. The result is heavy friction, causing the ground to shake as the plates slip.

In California, the Pacific coastal plate is diving below the North American continental plate. In the Mediterranean Basin, the African continental plate is crawling beneath the European plate.

A volcano forms as the leading edge of the submerging plate comes into contact with the molten layer of Earth's mantle, and the plate melts into magma. Some of its molten material is then forced up through cracks back to the surface. This can occur slowly or suddenly causing violent eruptions, spewing molten rock, ash, and gases high into the air and far away from the mountain.

The other two regions, in South Africa and Australia, sit atop much older geologic foundations. They are much more tectonically stable and have endured a much longer period of weathering. As a result, the landscape amid the mallee scrub is relatively flat and featureless.

Slippery Soils

Plants in the mediterranean scrub have to contend with a very stressful environment. Drought conditions in the summer and wildfires in the spring and fall are just two of the difficulties they must overcome in order to survive.

Another environmental factor is loose soils. Most soils are coarse-grained and prone to slippage on the slopes that most scrub formations grow on. In California, the slopes are steeper than most. Chaparral plants do a good job of taking root and holding on, keeping the soils in place and reaching deep down to find water.

Sometimes, finding that water and holding on to the soil are extremely difficult. Organic chemicals in some of the fallen leaves of chaparral plants are water-resistant; they form a barrier that keeps water from seeping into the soil.

Couple this with fire, and things get even more complicated. When the leaf litter burns, these chemicals vaporize (turn to gas) and move down into the soil layers, where they adhere to soil particles. This forms a water-repellent layer belowground that is parallel to the soil surface.

When rain falls, the soil absorbs it down to the water-repellent layer. The water cannot penetrate any farther, so it runs off downslope, carrying the surface soil and any nutrients along with it. This is one of the causes of landslides in the California chaparral formation. All this soil-filled water runs off down into the streams, causing floods, changing the shape of the streambeds, and smothering fish eggs and insect larvae.

Scrub vegetation is often the only thing holding soils back from eroding into streams and seas. Renosterveld even grows among dunes in South Africa's Cape region, shown here in De Hoop Nature Reserve.

SCRUB PLANTS

The plants that are adapted to the mediterranean climate have evolved forms that help them to survive the low water and nutrient levels. The shrub cover of scrub habitats tends to be from 3 to 16 feet (1 to 5 m) tall and grows very densely, with interlocking branches.

Many of the woody evergreen plants also have sclerophyllous leaves. This word comes from the Greek words *scleros*, meaning hard, and *phyllon*, meaning leaf. These hard leaves help to prevent wilting, contain flammable oils, and are resistant to decay. They are also very small, an adaptation that helps the plants retain moisture better than they could with larger leaves.

In summer, plants enter a period of dormancy. Their growth slows because of the lack of moisture, and their stomata—the pores that allow plants to expel oxygen and excess water vapor—close up to prevent water loss. Holding on to their leaves during the dormant season allows them to be ready to take advantage of infrequent summer rains by opening their stomata and photosynthesizing.

Many scrub plants have hard, waxy leaves to prevent moisture loss. Another tactic, shown here by this succulent plant in a California chaparral community, is to store water in thick, fleshy leaves.

Many scrub plants of the Mediterranean Basin have become some of the world's most popular cooking herbs because they are so aromatic. Plants like sage, oregano, thyme, and rosemary add strong flavors to many different foods.

The aboveground part of most scrub plants is only a small part of the whole plant. The root systems can be very extensive, a necessary adaptation in such a dry, unstable environment. The roots need to hold the plant in place in the loose soils, as well as cover a lot of area to get the necessary water and nutrients for the plant to survive. The root system of a 3-foot-tall (1-m-tall) plant may extend up to 49 feet (15 m) below ground.

Some species, such as red bloodwood, a mallee eucalyptus plant, have thick rhizomes and lignotubers, which help to store water and nutrients. If the aboveground part of the plant is destroyed by fire, the thick lignotuber, protected from fire by a layer of soil, can send out shoots again from buds concealed under the woody bark.

Other plants, called annuals, spread mainly by seed. If they are killed by fire, seeds that have spread in previous seasons and until now lain dormant in the soil, can sprout after the fire has passed. Some plants even need the intense heat of the fire to crack open the casings around their seeds before they can sprout.

Many species of scrub plants, especially chaparral shrubs, produce large bunches of small flowers throughout the rainy season rather than at one opportune time. Most of these shrubs are pollinated by various species of insects, which hatch out at different times so as not to overwhelm their food source. This insures that as many individuals of a given species will have as much to eat as possible when they most need it—at their crucial development stage. It also indirectly ensures that all the different species of insects will not be competing for the same food source.

Many Chilean matorral plants grow in clumps with bare spaces between them. This Chilean sorrel produces large blooms.

The drier the climate is, the sparser and smaller the vegetation becomes, creating a more open landscape. Eventually, the habitats become more desert-like. With increasing moisture, scrub habitats gradually change into woodlands and even forests.

Changes in vegetation also occur as the mineral content of the soil changes. As soils become poorer in nutrients and more acidic, another type of shrubland called heathlands take over. With increased fertility in the soil, grasslands and savannas become more common.

SCRUB ANIMALS

The animals of mediterranean shrublands are not as specifically adapted to the environment as the plants are. Many of these animals can and do exist outside of this biome. However, because the five expressions of mediterranean scrub are on different continents, most of the animals are specific to each region.

Some of the most important animals in shrubland communities are the ones that most people never see, the burrowing animals. These include mammals such as moles, pocket gophers, and other herbivorous rodents, as well as insects, such as termites. Burrowing animals are partly responsible for the diversity of these shrublands.

These creatures live underground, and their daily movements are responsible for moving soil from lower levels to the surface as they make their tunnels. This can provide plants with a unique place to colonize, as the richer soil is better for some plants than for others. Burrowing rodents also affect where plants grow because they often feed on the underground plant parts, such as roots.

Rodents are important to mediterranean scrub biomes for other reasons as well. They serve as food for some of the larger carnivores, such as foxes, coyotes, and birds of prey, or raptors.

Reptiles are relatively common in mediterranean shrublands as well, since they are better adapted to warmer, drier climates than mammals are. They feed mostly on the insect life that inhabits the scrub.

NATURAL FIRE

The same oils that help keep a plant's leaves from drying up during the arid mediterranean summers also make the plant highly vulnerable to fire. Ecologists actually think that these oils evolved in mediterranean shrubs in order to encourage fire.

Fires in these shrub communities occur on a periodic basis. In the case of California chaparral, they occur at least every five years in different locations within the formation. Some locations may not burn for many years, up to sixty or more.

Autumn brings the first rainstorms for some of these shrublands. The lightning that these storms spawn can often spark fires in the tinder-dry vegetation. Chaparral plants, in California, and mallee eucalyptus, in Australia, are particularly fire-prone. As soon as the fire is ignited, it spreads quickly, fueled by the dense growth, very dry litter on the ground, and the flammable oils in the leaves.

These hot fires sweep up scrub-covered hillsides, quickly consuming most of the aboveground branches and leaves. Most fires occur in late summer or autumn, when some scrub plants are dormant. A large

Fires in most scrub formations are common and natural events that help to regenerate the plant life. Some seeds need the heat of the fire in order to sprout and begin their growth.

percentage of a dormant plant's energy reserves are stored as carbohydrates in their root systems. When a fire or other natural disaster destroys their branches and leaves, these plants still have the energy they need underground to resprout, sending up new shoots during the following growing season. Some plants have buds just under the bark along their stems, while others—such as manzanita and chamise, two typical chaparral plants—sprout from the base or the root stock, .

After the fire has consumed all the tangled growth, it leaves behind ash that enriches the soil. Sunlight can now reach the ground and, along with winter rains, helps to create excellent conditions for new plant growth. Many seeds are stored in the soil, waiting for this opportunity. These plants, such as snowbrush, are truly fire-adapted plants. Their seeds can stay in the soil for up to 575 years, ready to sprout after a fire.

Other plants mature and flower within five to eight years, the typical time span between fires. They flower abundantly the first season after a fire. When the seeds form from the flower and are spread throughout the area, they come to rest in the soil to wait for the next fire. Some seeds are stimulated to sprout not from the heat of the fire, but from organic chemicals that leach into the soil from the charred wood.

Another group of plants, known as perennials, which die back every year and sprout again from bulbs during the next growing season, also flower more after a fire.

While animals in scrub communities are not as well-adapted to fire as plants are, they have ways of avoiding the heat, smoke, and flames. Burrowing rodents are often protected from the fire by the layer of soil above them, while some reptiles hole up in crevices between rocks. Larger, more mobile animals can simply run away.

Within six years after a fire in chaparral communities, the shrubs have closed in again, creating a dense, impenetrable stand; until the next lightning strike, that is.

Fire burning in chaparral and other natural plant communities can threaten homes built within and near these ecosystems, such as this fire burning in desert and an inland form of chaparral in Arizona.

3

A MAN-MADE BIOME

Humans have lived among the mediterranean shrublands for thousands of years, and in a sense, we have evolved with them, altering the landscape to suit our needs. Many of the world's largest cities—Los Angeles, Rome, Tunis, Santiago, Cape Town—can be found in the mediterranean regions. In some cases, the current condition of a particular shrubland is maintained by the practices of man. Other shrublands are degrading because of human activities. This is why mediterranean scrub habitats are considered globally rare.

AGRICULTURE AND GRAZING

Because of their mild climate and proximity to large bodies of water, many of the world's mediterranean regions have become important centers of agriculture. Many areas around the Mediterranean Basin have been cultivated for thousands of years. Some cultivated crops have become wild again, such as olive and carob trees.

California's Central Valley, a former scrub habitat, is one of the most productive agricultural areas in the United States, providing a wide variety of fruits and vegetables for the nation. Australian farmers have planted extensive wheat fields in areas formerly covered with mallee eucalyptus scrub. And much of the scrub region around Cape Town, South Africa, was long ago converted into grain fields and vineyards.

The foothills of the coast range and the Vallee Central in central Chile was first converted to farms by the Incan peoples. Later, Spanish colonists took over the area, putting the natives to work as slaves, enabling them to cultivate even greater amounts of land.

Areas that were not used for farming were cut and burned to allow grasses to grow as fodder for livestock, such as sheep, goats, alpacas, and llamas. This practice has created a patchy landscape of various imported and native grasses among shrubby plants that are too dense, unpalatable, or even poisonous for the livestock to eat.

This patchy landscape—garrigue in southern Europe, jaral in Chile—is kept in its current state by grazing cattle. If the grazing stopped, the plant community might change to another type.

INVASIVE SPECIES

Not only has each individual formation of mediterranean scrub been affected by human activities, but each one has been influenced by the others through the actions of humans. People have long moved between these regions, carrying their favorite plants and animals with them to their new homes, causing significant changes to scrub ecosystems.

The biggest change has been the introduction of plants from the Mediterranean Basin to all the other formations. Many of the native grasses and herbs of the Chilean and Californian shrublands have been replaced by ones from the Mediterranean Basin. These species have been evolving with grazing animals in the Mediterranean for a very long

After people introduced the European rabbit into different parts of the world—including the mallee scrub—the rabbits' populations exploded, causing major environmental damage.

time, and so have adapted to tolerate these pressures. This makes these plants more adaptable to varying conditions.

The European rabbit has spread wildly in Australia and central Chile since its introduction to both these locations in the nineteenth century. With no natural predators to stop its spread, the populations of these rabbits quickly grew.

The rodent was introduced in southern Victoria, Australia, in 1859 as a game species for hunters. Within ten years it became a pest in this region, and it soon spread throughout the rest of the country. Control measures have been attempted ever since. Today it is still Australia's number-one pest species.

HUMAN-CAUSED FIRE

For a long time, people have used fire as a tool for more than just keeping warm. Aboriginal Australians and Native Americans used fire to encourage the growth of favored plants. They harvested the seeds and other plant parts that resprouted after fire. Another benefit was the game animals, such as deer and kangaroos, that came to feed on this fresh, young growth. These animals were much easier to hunt this way.

There is also evidence that early peoples used fire to reduce the dangerous buildup of fuels—dead wood and leaves—in the woodlands, forest, and grasslands. Fires that occur naturally in late summer and early autumn tend to burn very hot since the fuels are very dry. Native people burned the chaparral and mallee earlier in the growing season, when plants and the ground were still moist. This allowed them to control the fire more easily and kept the fires from burning out of control.

The burning continued after Europeans settled many of these regions, such as Chile and California. The Spaniards learned from the native peoples who burned the scrub to encourage the grasses and herbs for their grazing cattle.

Fire was never an important element in the central Chilean matorral because summer lightning storms rarely penetrated the region beyond the coastal mountains. Much of the shrub formation that now grows in central Chile used to be occupied by woodland and forests. Clearing for

Fire has never naturally been a large influence on the Chilean matorral, but its introduction by people now keeps the formation from gradually changing into forest.

agriculture caused a change to shrubland, and more frequent burning maintained it. If fires were stopped, the vegetation would likely return to forest.

As the human population increased and people began settling in fire-prone areas, a policy of fire suppression was adopted in some parts of the world. All fires, natural or human-caused, were extinguished.

In the United States during the twentieth century, this policy led to a dangerous buildup of dead wood, leaves, and other flammable organic matter. In areas where fires were allowed to burn, this material was consumed gradually in smaller surface fires.

When this material builds up to dangerous levels, fires called ground fires burn hotter and can penetrate deeper down into the soil layer, consuming roots and killing vegetation that ordinarily would have been able to resprout from rootstock.

In dense woodland and forest, fires can climb trees using "ladder fuels," shrubs, small trees, and low branches—burning all the way up to the canopies. These crown fires, as they are known, spread quickly from tree to tree and can do much more damage than a surface fire.

In mediterranean scrub communities, humans have altered natural fire cycles, increasing or decreasing the frequency of fires. This change in timing and intensity of fires has often caused a change in vegetation. If fires occur more frequently, many plants cannot take root at all, causing the soil to become loose and to be washed away in heavy rains.

Suppressing fires causes a buildup of fuels, changing the timing and type of fires from frequent, mild surface fires to infrequent, catastrophic wildfires, which consume all the aboveground and much of the belowground plant material. These fires with a lot of fuel are a great danger to people and structures as they burn very hot and unpredictably. Many houses built in the mountains of Southern California have been consumed by these exceptionally hot fires.

Renosterveld, part of a larger unrelated group of South African shrublands called fynbos, is the closest equivalent to other formations of Mediterranean scrub.

4

AFRICAN AND AUSTRALIAN SCRUB

African and Australian formations of mediterranean shrubland are the most unusual of all. They are both geologically much older, receive more rainfall, grow on flatter land with poorer soils, and are more biologically diverse than any other formations.

RENOSTERVELD

At the very southern tip of the African continent, in the Cape Province, lie both the city of Cape Town, the legislative capital of South Africa, and the local regional formation of mediterranean scrub. The entire Cape region is known to plant scientists as the Cape Floristic Kingdom, one of six divisions of the world based on floral diversity. The scrub part of the Cape Kingdom is considered the most biologically diverse of all the mediterranean shrubland formations. As with Australia, most of the flora here is of tropical origin, but it has adapted to the mediterranean climate.

Rain occurs frequently in the winter, from May to September, in the cape region. Unlike typical mediterranean climates, rain does fall here in the summer, although for only a few days each month. Winds are nearly constant here as well, which contributes to the dry conditions of this formation.

There are many different shrublands in the Cape Province, but renosterveld is the formation that most closely resembles Earth's other four mediterranean scrub regions. Coastal renosterveld lies along the coastal lowlands at the foot of the various rugged sandstone mountain ranges, known as the Coastal Folded Belt, that line the western and southern boundaries of the Cape. Mountain renosterveld occurs higher up, along the mountain slopes.

There is often no clear divide between the different types of shrubland in South Africa. Renosterveld exists not only on its own, but it also mixes in with another, more widespread type of shrubland called fynbos. Fynbos are considered to be heathlands and so do not fit the definition of mediterranean scrub. Fynbos occupy more than half of the areas of mediterranean climate in South Africa, while renosterveld occupies about a third.

Plants

Renosterveld is an Afrikaans word meaning "rhinoceros veld." It was probably named at a time when the black rhinoceros, now an endangered species, used to roam the scrub. The dominant plant of the formation, called renosterbos, is a member of the daisy family. It can grow up to 3 feet (1 m) tall and has been used by native Africans as fuel for stoves and as medication for stomach problems.

About 1,000 species of plants grow in the renosterveld, including members of the pea, thyme, cocoa, and gardenia families. Most plants have tough, small, gray leaves. Rensoterveld is especially rich in the number and species of perennials, such as irises, lilies, and orchids.

Coastal renosterveld is made up of a layer of low shrubs, 3 to 5 feet (1 to 1.5 m) tall and, below this, a layer of grasses and perennials. Some of the more common shrubs growing beneath the rensoterbos are wild rosemary and dune teabush. Larger shrubs, up to 10 feet (3 m) tall, sometimes poke above the renosterbos and lower shrubs.

Much of the land formerly occupied by coastal renosterveld is now taken up with wheat fields. Historically, this scrub formation may have been an even more diverse plant community than it is now. Europeans used the land heavily for grazing, burning it regularly, likely causing some plants to go locally extinct. Renosterbos and grasses are more common now because of that practice.

Mountain renosterveld is made up of many of the same plants as the coastal type, but it grows on different soils and at higher elevations farther inland. This type is more open and often grows in drier, rockier

Bitter aloe is a common plant in the mountain form of renosterveld. Many animals make use of the nectar and flowers of this plant.

soils. Renosterbos is the dominant plant here as well, but there are fewer grasses and a greater number of succulents, plants that store water in their thick, fleshy leaves. Shrub plants include bitter aloe, used widely for medicinal purposes, and sweet thorn.

Renosterveld plants that grow along the south coast tend to be taller and grow more densely than their west coast counterparts. The south coast generally receives more rainfall in the summer than the west coast does.

Animals

When the renosterveld formations were much more widespread, they supported a diversity of large mammals. Grazing animals such as mountain zebra, eland, red-hartebeest, buffalo, elephant, and black rhinoceros once roamed among the renosterbos. Many carnivores hunted these and other smaller mammals, but very few leopards, cheetahs, lions, or spotted hyenas are left in the region.

As the renosterveld was being cleared for farms, many of these animals were hunted or driven away into the mountains. Some exist only within wildlife sanctuaries today. The quagga, a horselike mammal with stripes on its head and neck, was hunted to extinction in the late nineteenth century.

Mammals that still exist in the renosterveld include a few species of antelopes in the mountain formation, including the Cape grysbok and the common duiker. Leopards also still roam the higher elevations, as well as aardvarks and honey badgers. Chacma baboons and molerats feast on the bulbs and tubers of the many perennial plants. The Cape spiny mouse and the Cape molerat are endemic to this area.

One of the most diverse groups of animals in the renosterveld and the fynbos are tortoises. Leopard and angulate tortoises, as well as the speckled padloper, are some of the more common tortoises found in

The common duiker, an antelope species, is found in renosterveld and other habitats in Sub-Saharan Africa.

the region. The geometric tortoise is endemic to the renosterveld and is considered endangered. Loss of habitat and replacement of native vegetation with inedible weeds have made life very difficult for this species.

Human History

South Africa has precious little of its historical mediterranean shrublands left—less than 5 percent. Clearing land for agriculture and urban development has replaced them, as it has in Australia. Cape Town, a city of three million people, lies on the western coast amidst lands formerly covered by scrub and heathlands.

There has been a long history of human activity in the western part of the country. Fire has been used to drive game animals and increase the growth of favored plants. People created grasslands for grazing animals by burning the shrub communities more frequently than the scrub plants could handle.

Scrub communities cover the hills above Fish Hoek, a small fishing village in the Western Cape of South Africa.

Today, many crops are grown on the fertile, fine-grained soils. Grapes are particularly successful, so vineyards and wineries are popular businesses here. Farmers and vintners still cut back or burn the woody vegetation to keep their fields open.

The natural fire regime has also been changed by the introduction of nonnative plant species, such as pine and acacia trees. These trees are adapted to fire and, like many fire-adapted plants, even encourage fire with the resins in their wood and leaves, as well as in the buildup of dry, flammable leaves and branches.

Not much of the remaining renosterveld is currently protected. Less than 1 percent of coastal renosterveld and less than 5 percent of mountain renosterveld have been set aside as conservation areas.

MALLEE SCRUB

In Australia, the mediterranean climate occurs along the southern coast of the continent, from western Victoria in the east to southwest Western Australia in the west. Rain falls mostly from April to October, but summer storms do occur, providing more rain during the dormant season than any other scrub formation receives. The mallee scrub is one of the most diverse mediterranean scrub formations in the world. In particular, it supports a wide variety of mammal and reptile species.

Plants

A diverse group of plant communities, from forest to heathland, grows in the mediterranean region of Australia. Mallee open scrub usually grows under the most extreme conditions, on soils that are waterlogged in the rainy season or on very shallow and rocky soils.

Mallee, a native Aboriginal word, refers to about 130 species of eucalyptus that take on a shrubby growth habit. Of these, only ten or

Like other mallee plants, the large-flowered mallee, a species of eucalyptus, grows from multiple stems. This species has a large flower and fruit.

twelve species are common in scrub formations. These grow as tall as 16 to 26 feet (5 to 8 m), so some are the size of small trees. Like other scrub shrubs, mallee eucalyptuses have dense leaves filled with very flammable oils.

Fires burn regularly in mallee scrub. Depending on the site, fires can occur in cycles of fifteen years up to more than one hundred. In these very hot fires, the branches and leaves of plants are normally killed, while the parts below the soil—rootstocks, rhizomes, and tubers— usually survive the crown fires and sprout new branches from dormant buds.

Plants growing beneath the mallee are usually grasses and herbs. In drier regions, succulents take over the understory. Many of the plants in mallee scrub are like other scrub plants all over the world in that they have adapted to grow mostly in the spring so they are ready to go dormant during the most stressful period of the year, the dry summer. Mallee eucalyptuses, however, are different—they start their yearly growth in the summer and continue into autumn.

Plant ecologists believe that this is because the eucalyptus evolved in a subtropical environment, where rain occurred on a more regular basis throughout the year. Mallee is probably a more recent addition to the scrub formation in Australia. The mallee plants are able to survive and prosper because they can utilize the water from occasional summer rains as well as the water stored in the soil from winter rains.

Animals

Australia is the only mediterranean scrub region where there are no burrowing rodents. Harvester termites are the main burrowing creatures here.

Feeding on these insects are the regions many marsupials as well as spiny anteaters and bats. Other mammals that use the mallee scrub include mice, cats, dingoes, and other creatures. Wallabies are some of the smallest grazing animals in the mallee scrub.

Many reptiles make the scrub their home, such as dragon lizards, goannas, skinks, legless lizards, and snakes—including worm snakes,

Wallabies are one of the many herbivores in the Australian mallee. The agile wallaby utilizes grasslands and forest as well as scrub for its grazing.

pythons, and a number of species of front-fanged snakes. Four species of burrowing frogs live in the region as well. They estivate during the hot, dry summers. This means that they burrow into the mud of wetlands so their skin won't dry out when the water evaporates.

Birds of the mallee are also very diverse, with more than 160 species, including honeyeaters, parrots and cockatoos, warblers, flycatchers, and many others. Only nine of these species are endemic to the mallee.

The regent parrot, an endemic species, nests in stands of eucalyptus trees and feeds on seeds of herbs and grasses in the lower levels of the mallee.This species is in decline because of the clearing of mallee scrub for agriculture.

Other endemic species include the southern scrub-robin, yellow-plumed honeyeater, purple-gaped honeyeater, mallee heath-wren, and the yellow-rumped pardalote. The red-lored whistler has a complex, haunting call. The black-eared miner, a species of honeyeater—birds that feed on nectar from plants—is considered endangered because it prefers mature mallee scrub for its habitat. Most of the existing scrub has been burned too frequently for it to reach maturity.

The purple-gaped honeyeater is a true mallee resident, feeding on the nectar from mallee eucalyptus flowers and other scrub plants.

Human History

Mediterranean scrub communities in Australia are much reduced from their historical extent. Clearing for agriculture after World War II has mostly eliminated them, since the lands they grow on are relatively flat and fertile. Many former mallee scrub communities are now covered with wheat fields and sheep pastures.

Australia used to be the top producer of eucalyptus oil in the world. The oil was harvested from the mallee scrub plants and used as an antibiotic for both animals and people. Farmers also used it to kill insects infesting their chickens and to keep the birds' feathers clean and fresh.

Soldiers returning from the war thought raising crops was more profitable than the long, difficult process of extracting eucalyptus oil from the mallee plants. Once the mallee scrub was torn up and the land planted with wheat or grazed with sheep, eucalyptus oil production dropped sharply, from 1,000 tons a year to about 150 tons.

Australian scientists and farmers have learned, however, that not only does the mallee eucalyptus provide a useful oil from its leaves, it also helps the soil. The thirsty roots absorb a lot of moisture from the salt-rich groundwater, holding the salts and diluting the water. With so much mallee removed, however, the water table has risen, bringing saltwater up closer to the surface. Wheat and other agricultural crops that normally rely on rainwater will die from long exposure to the salty water.

Farmers have replanted more than twenty million eucalyptus trees in Western Australia in an attempt to lower the ground water levels. Researchers are also studying whether reforestation will help the existing patches of natural mallee scrub, which are also damaged by excess salt levels in the groundwater.

Some of the remaining areas of natural mallee scrub are very small but are managed as public recreation and conservation lands, such as those around the Murray River in Victoria.

While most North American formations of chaparral occur in California, moister desert areas—especially in river valleys—can support forms of chaparral, such as along the Rio Grande River valley in New Mexico.

5

SCRUB HABITATS IN THE AMERICAS

Although separated in geological history, the mediterranean scrub formations in California and Chile have evolved to become the most similar of the shrubland communities. They are both relatively young systems, from their geology to their plant life and human history.

Their topography, or terrain, is also very similar. California chaparral and Chilean matorral formations both lie on the west (Pacific) coasts of their continents. Each has two mountain ranges that run parallel to the coastline, their interior range topped with very tall, jagged peaks.

The climate is also similar in the two locations, with the greatest amount of rain falling in the winter. Fog forming from warming ocean air rolls in on a regular basis in the summer to keep the land semi-moist. Chile receives more rain than California, however, and has a milder climate overall.

Both the matorral and the chaparral are bordered on the equator side by desert and on the pole side by temperate forest. While the plants and animals of both places have evolved from temperate and tropical ancestors, the types and species of plants that grow in both of these scrub formations are very different. Chilean matorral plants are more similar to Australian and African shrubland types, while California chaparral plants are more similar to those found in the Mediterranean Basin.

The human history of the chaparral and the matorral is also similar. Both regions were long used by native peoples, and Spaniards were the first Europeans to colonize both California and Chile.

CALIFORNIA CHAPARRAL

The chaparral formation of California grows along the Pacific coast of North America from Oregon in the north to Baja California in the south. It stretches east, across the Coast, Transverse, and Peninsular Mountain Ranges, through the Central Valley, and into the Sierra Nevada Mountains.

The most extensive areas of chaparral grow in Southern California on steep slopes up to 6,500 feet (2,000 m) in elevation. Typically dense

The Santa Monica Mountains are covered in a blanket of chaparral, the most extensive formation in California.

stands blanket the hillsides. It is often found mixed in with other plant communities, such as oak woodland or grassland.

Frequent summer rainstorms spawn lightning that can ignite the tinder-dry hillsides of chaparral. Since chaparral covers such large areas, these fires can burn quickly, consuming up to tens of thousands of acres of vegetation.

Foehn winds, known locally in southern California as Santa Ana winds, blow in spring and autumn from the deserts in the east. These winds bring very hot and dry air that increases the aridity of the already parched chaparral. Dry conditions increase the number and intensity of dangerous wildfires at this time of the year.

The word *chaparral* is originally derived from a Basque word, *txapar*, meaning thicket. The Spanish changed this to *chaparro*, the name for the areas of evergreen scrub oak that grow in mediterranean shrub communities in southern Spain. This word was also used to name chaps, the leggings that cowboys wear to protect their legs as they ride on horseback through the dense scrub.

Plants

The dominant plants in the chaparral community are stunted shrubs that grow to only 3 to 13 feet (1 to 4 m) tall. There are more than 240 species of shrubs that grow here, but, depending upon the conditions, usually fewer than twenty are found in a given location. They grow densely with crooked, interlocking branches, making it almost impossible to move through this scrub.

On drier sites, species of chamise, an evergreen shrub with short, needlelike leaves, and manzanita, a twisted, woody, red-barked plant, dominate the plant cover. Their leaves are sclerophyllous, like many other mediterranean scrub plants, so they can resist drying out and can photosynthesize all year round.

Pine trees mix with the California coastal sage scrub chaparral. At higher elevations, the pine trees grow more densely.

The moister sites allow more diverse plant communities, made up of scrub oaks, toyon, hollyleaf cherry, mountain mahogany, and laurel sumac. A slightly different form, montane chaparral, grows at higher elevations. It mixes with forest and woodlands of coniferous trees and can replace these communities if a fire kills them.

Coastal sage scrub, a form of scrub with shrubs that lose their leaves in summer, grows along the coast. California sagebrush and bush sunflower are the dominant plants. Succulents and cacti are also common here.

The plants of the coastal sage scrub are more shallowly rooted than inland chaparral plants. Moisture from the regularly occurring fog provides most of these plants' water needs. This plant community is considered one the most endangered ecosystems in North America, with many endemic species, including the San Diego barrel cactus and the San Diego thorn mint.

Other plant forms also grow within the chaparral communities, including trees, vines, and herbs. Annual plants provide a very showy display of flowers during the first spring after a fire burns out the shrubs. The seeds of some of these plants are cued to sprout when the heat from the fires cracks open their seed casings. Other plants have seeds that sprout in response to chemicals leached out of the burnt wood.

Fires also influence the forms that plants take in the chaparral. Many species sprout from lignotubers or burls at a plant's base after a fire. Plants can survive for a very long time being burned back and resprouting again and again. The main growth is added to the burls, and these can develop into a platform-like base as much as 13 feet (4 m) wide and can live for more than 250 years. This recurrent killing and sprouting is what gives chaparral plants their multistemmed, crooked forms.

Wildfires can, and often do, change the type of plant community that grows in a particular spot. If fires occur frequently—every five to ten years, for example—grasslands may take over. If fires in the chaparral are suppressed, a stunted forest of live oaks or a mixture of oaks and grassland may take its place.

Chaparral plants are very important for watershed protection. They hold the hillside soils in place. If heavy rains follow soon after a wildfire sweeps through an area, landslides may result since the vegetation is no longer there to deflect and absorb the rain.

Animals

In chaparral communities, there is very high diversity among some animal groups. Insects are numerous in the coastal sage scrub. There are 150 to 200 species of butterflies, for example, including the Quino checkerspot butterfly. This formation also hosts the greatest diversity of endemic bees in the United States. These bees thrive on the nectar from

The California ground squirrel spends most of its time on the ground, feeding on seeds, nuts, leaves, and roots of plants. It also spends time underground in its burrows, which it shares with other ground squirrels.

the many flowering plants and serve to pollinate them as well.

Some of the most numerous animals in the chaparral are the rodents, including the California ground squirrel, the California mouse, and the California pocket mouse. Brush rabbits are also common. The soil beneath many chaparral stands are riddled with the tunnels of the valley pocket gopher.

The tunnels, which the gophers use to find food (the roots of plants), and seek out mates, provide a great service to the chaparral community. In the process of excavating these tunnels, the gophers pile up the soil at defunct tunnel entrances. The freshly turned soils from lower down in the soil profile are richer in minerals than the soils at the surface. These piles serve as perfect sites for different species of plants to colonize, which increases the overall plant diversity.

While the Santa Cruz kangaroo rat is not listed as endangered by the United States or the state of California, its populations have seriously declined in the last twenty-five years. This decline has caused changes in the vegetation of the chaparral. Like the valley pocket gopher, the kangaroo rat moves soil and seeds around, affecting the numbers and distribution of plants. Some area where these rodents no longer live are changing to grassland.

Where there are rodents, there are bound to be snakes. The gopher snake makes a good living preying upon the various small rodents that scurry through the dense brush. Endangered reptile species include the coastal horned lizard and the orange-throated whiptail lizard.

Some animals only use the chaparral for part of the year. The beautifully marked mountain quail, for example, lives in chaparral during the winter, then moves to higher elevations for the summer months. This local migration is all done on foot, sometimes covering a distance of 20 miles (32 kilometers).

The wrentit is a fairly common bird in California chaparral and coastal sage scrub. The California thrasher and the California gnatcatcher are two other birds that are strongly associated with chaparral and are listed as endangered. The densely growing shrubs provide excellent cover and nesting sites for these birds.

Human History

Only in recent times have humans begun to build houses and live among chaparral communities in California. Native Americans lived at lower elevations and only used the chaparral as hunting and gathering grounds, burning it to encourage plant growth and game animals.

Natural fires in the chaparral have been suppressed, or extinguished, for most of the twentieth century to protect expensive homes built in these areas. In California today, humans cause many of the fires that occur in the chaparral. As a result, fires are occurring more frequently and changing the composition of the vegetation. Fires that occur frequently in the same area can also lead to the destruction of entire areas indirectly through landslides.

Prescribed fire is a land management tool that is used to both maintain these types of fire-dependent communities and to reduce the risk of catastrophic wildfires. Many prescribed fires are conducted in the late fall, when soils are moist and the danger of natural fire is passed. These fires don't burn as hot as summer burns. This is unfortunate because the seeds of many fire-adapted plants in the chaparral only maintain their resistance to intense heat during the period when the risk is greatest, during the natural fire cycle of late summer and early fall. Their resistance to heat drops after this point, so ironically, burning in the late fall can destroy many fire-adapted seeds.

Chaparral grows in what has become one of the most expensive real estate areas in the United States. As a result, much of the scrub has been removed for agriculture and development of housing and golf courses. Coastal sage scrub in particular is highly endangered and exists only in small patches.

CHILEAN MATORRAL

Central Chile has a long history of human use. Prior to this use, the region was most likely covered in forests, not shrublands. Today, the matorral grows amidst farms, national parks, cities, and towns. Santiago, Chile's capital, populated by five million people, is within the region defined as matorral.

Much like California, Central Chile's topography is very mountainous. The coastal range, or Cordillera de la Costa, rises to a height of 7,150 feet (2,200 m) at El Roble peak, and is separated by the Vallee Central from the larger mountain range to the west. The Andean Cordillera, or Andes Mountains, attain heights up to 22,750 feet (7,000 m).

Western Fence Lizards

Different animals have found their own special ways of dealing with a landscape that burns frequently, such as chaparral. Many different seed-eating birds take advantage of the exposed ground after a fire to feed on the seeds in the soil, while raptors—hawks, falcons, eagles, and vultures—feed on the rodents and reptiles that no longer have the plants for cover. Mule deer populations increase in areas that are growing back after burning. The fresh young growth provides the deer with ample forage.

Western fence lizards normally find cover in crevices in rocky areas, but when a fire removes the vegetation, they become even more exposed and vulnerable as they search for food. Since the color of the lizards matches the grayish color of the standing burnt stems, these smart lizards perch at the tips, blending right in. This camouflage helps them to avoid raptors, coyotes, foxes, and other predators. If they are discovered, they can quickly take cover in the dense new growth under the dead stems.

The scrub-covered foothills below the Torres del Paine Mountains surround a small pond here in the Chilean matorral.

The rivers in California flow north to south, parallel to the Central Valley and the mountain ranges, while the rivers in Chile flow from west to east, cutting through the coastal range. They can do this because the upper layers of rock in the Andes are made of sedimentary rock, which erodes much more quickly than other rock types. These broken-down rocks and soils are carried by rains down into the Vallee Central. As a result, most mountain soils are shallow and not well developed.

Plants

The Chilean matorral is more diverse than California chaparral, both in the type of plant life, and in the structure of the vegetation. There are fewer unbroken stands of matorral scrub vegetation; typical matorral is clumped, with openings and grassy areas amidst the shrubs. The plants also grow at multiple layers, with small trees at the top, shrubs beneath, and grasses at the ground level. These stands grow along the slopes of the coast range and in the foothills of the Andes.

There are many succulents and spiny cacti in the matorral, which probably discourages herbivores. Since spiny plants don't have leaves, photosynthesis takes place in their green stems.

Many herbs grow beneath matorral shrubs, which is unusual for scrub formations. Some of these plants are bulb-forming lilies and irises, as well as ferns and vinelike plants.

A coastal version of the typical matorral formation grows on dunes and ocean bluffs near the coast. At higher elevations in the Andes, between 3,900 and 4,900 feet (1,200 and 1,500 m), matorral shrubs don't get as tall as those in lowland formations, but some may grow to tree size.

Plants in the matorral number near 2,000 species, compared to about 900 in the chaparral. Most of the native plants are endemics, growing only in Chile. The Chilean palm is a threatened species with a very limited range. It has been harvested for its syrup and nuts, and now it only exists in national parks.

Wildflowers grow among the cacti and succulents of the matorral, more common here than in the chaparral.

Animals

Animal diversity is nowhere near as great as plant diversity in the Chilean matorral. Some species, like the Chilean mockingbird, only live here. Other species use the matorral only for some of their needs. The giant hummingbird is the largest hummingbird in the world, at 8.5 inches (21.7 cm). It spends just the spring and summer in the matorral. Reptiles are more diverse than mammals, and many species of swift live here.

Most plant-eating animals in Chile were introduced by settlers. Alpacas and llamas were brought to the region by the Incas after the guanaco, a native grazer, was eliminated by hunting.

Rabbits and hares were also introduced from Europe and now run wild in great numbers across the landscape since they have no natural predators to keep their numbers down.

The largest hummingbird in the world, the giant hummingbird, breeds in the Chilean matorral and will even nest in cacti.

Human History

Along with the Mediterranean Basin, Chile has sustained some of the greatest impacts from humans. The vegetation that exists now in the central Chilean matorral is the result of human modification dating back 10,000 years.

The Incan people practiced agriculture and kept livestock—llamas and alpacas. As a result, they cleared much of the region for farms, pasture, firewood, and building materials. They also burned the fields each autumn to clear them of brush.

These practices, especially grazing, intensified after the Spaniards colonized the area in the sixteenth century. All but the most inaccessible land was used, so that, by the early nineteenth century, most of the matorral had been eliminated. Humans still use the land heavily, and as a result, the vegetation is maintained in a modified condition, shrubby and open.

As a result of this constant pressure on the landscape, tree species, like the litre tree, became adapted to life as shrubs. If these impacts were reduced or eliminated, the shrub communities of the Chilean matorral would revert to forests and woodlands.

The Chilean government has also planted thousands of non-native trees on the slopes of the coast range in order to stabilize the soils. This reduces the habitat for matorral shrubs.

Fire plays a much smaller role in the Chilean matorral than in other mediterranean shrublands. Central Chile's moister climate, forest history, and less fire-prone vegetation all play a role in reducing the incidence of fire. Thunderstorms do not occur in the matorral in the summer, so lightning is rare, and there are no foehn-type winds that dry out other scrub formations. Any fire in the matorral is human-caused. Because most matorral plant species are not adapted to fire, they may die off if large, frequent, and intense fires are introduced into the landscape.

Scrub grows densely and on steep slopes along the Mediterranean Sea, as shown here in the Sierra Nevada in Spain.

6

MEDITERRANEAN BASIN SCRUB

The actual Mediterranean Basin scrub region, the one for which all other mediterranean shrubland formations are named, is also the largest. Calling it one region, however, is not all that accurate. Stretching 2,360 miles (3,800 km) from the Atlantic Ocean to the Middle East, this region spans three continents and many countries.

Each country, and sometimes each region or culture within each country, has their own name for the shrublands that make up this formation. In fact, there is so much variety within this large region that there are dozens of scrub types that fit into the definition of mediterranean shrubland.

However, all types can be grouped within the broad category called matorral, the Spanish word also used to name the Chilean scrub formation. In France there are two types, called *maquis* and *garrigue,* and in Italy the names are similar—*macchia* and *gariga*. In Spain they are called *matorral* and *tomillares*, in Greece and Turkey, *phrygana*, and in Israel, *maquis* and *choresh*.

RING OF SCRUB

The long west-east configuration of the 1.2 million-square-mile (3,000,000 km²) Mediterranean Sea allows the drying trade winds that create the mediterranean climate to penetrate deeply to the east, making this the most extensive region of mediterranean shrubland in the world.

This large inland sea is nearly surrounded along its entire 28,600 miles (46,000 km) of coastline by tall, rugged mountains, including the Sierra Nevada in Spain, the Atlas Mountains in Morocco, the Alpes Maritimes in France, the Apennines in Italy, the Pindus in Greece, the Taurus in Turkey, and the Dinaric Alps along the Balkan Peninsula. The Greek Islands are a chain of undersea mountains whose tops stick above the waterline.

Scrub formations are found in the lowlands and on the foothills of these mountain ranges. The whole region can be divided into two halves, western and eastern, with the divide stretching along a raised sill in the Mediterranean Sea between the Italian island of Sicily and Tunisia in North Africa. To the west, the plant and animal life has similarities with that of central Europe, while to the east, the ties to central Asia are more apparent.

Winds from the south dry out the region in summer, while cold winds from the north sweep the area in winter. Foehn winds occasionally blow in from the Sahara Desert on the African continent in spring, wilting crops and leaving a film of dust everywhere.

Fortunately, rain does fall in the summer, but very irregularly. The northwestern part of the region receives more rain than the eastern part. Most rainstorms happen between November and April, and they can often be severe, dropping a lot of water quickly, causing erosion.

More than any other scrub formations, those encircling the Mediterranean Basin have evolved closely with humans and so are maintained and heavily influenced by their activities.

Taller shrubs grow in the maquis formation, shown here along the coast of Greece.

MAQUIS AND GARRIGUE

Maquis and garrigue are the two main types of mediterranean scrub. These formations are mostly composed of a dense layer of low shrubs, with a ground cover of herbs and, in some places, an upper layer of small trees.

Maquis usually colonizes areas where forest once grew. After these areas are cleared of trees and left alone, these shrubs establish themselves and form a dense cover. Maquis is the tallest of the mediterranean shrubland formations in this region, reaching heights of 16 to 20 feet (5 to 6 m).

Garrigue is a lower-growing form, usually less than 3 feet (1 m) tall. It grows less densely than maquis, with patches of bare ground between clusters of shrubs, grasses, and herbs. Olive trees grow both cultivated and wild in these formations. Many of the region's most prized cooking herbs, such as rosemary, thyme, and oregano, grow wild here. Bright, beautiful flowers color the hillsides in April and provide food for honeybees. Mediterranean honey is widely cultivated and considered to be of very high quality.

Plants

The plant life of the Mediterranean matorral is very diverse, with roughly 25,000 species. However, since the Mediterranean Basin contains such a larger area of scrub, the actual diversity averages out to be about the same as the other formations.

Some of the more common and dominant species in the maquis are holm and kermes oaks. These plants are very hardy and can withstand

This strawberry tree, a common Mediterranean shrub, displays both flowers and fruits at the same time.

Rock rose grows well in the garrigue and other mediterranean scrub formations because it can tolerate dry soils and windy conditions.

intense heat, cold, and drought. Another important adaptation is their ability to resprout after fire.

The leaves of these oaks are very spiny, so much so that only goats are able to eat them. In fact, grazing by goats is the main reason that these oaks grow as shrub species—normally, they grow as trees. So these oaks can be grazed, cut, and burned, and they still come back strong. Some have been known to live 700 years.

Other tree species are carob and lentisk. Carob is a member of the pea family and grows long, wide, brown seed pods that look like large pea pods. The seeds are used as feed for cattle, as food thickeners, and even ground and used as a substitute for cocoa. The lentisk, or mastic tree, can grow as a tree with a maximum height of 26 feet (8 m), but normally it grows as a low, spreading shrub. The resin from this plant is used to make chewing gum.

Rock-roses, also native to the region, are popular among gardeners for their showy flowers. A group of plants called brooms are deciduous, but they can grow all year round because they have green stems that absorb sunlight.

The bee orchid has evolved to look like a female bee, which attracts male bees who then carry the pollen from one flower to another, effectively pollinating the plants.

Orchids

Orchids are a widespread and unusual group of plants found throughout the world, but mostly in tropical regions. There are anywhere from 20,000 to 35,000 species worldwide. They vary in size and shape. Most orchids produce beautiful, showy flowers with three petals, one of which is shaped differently than the others.

More than one hundred species of orchids also grow in the Mediterranean matorral. Whereas other species of orchids that grow in the temperate zone prefer sheltered, shady, forested locations, the scrub orchids prefer warm, exposed conditions.

The openness of the habitat allows the butterflies and solitary bees that pollinate them to see the flowers over great distances. Orchids take on their unusual forms in order to attract insects or birds so that these creatures may carry pollen to another orchid, which helps the plants reproduce.

Since it has no nectar, the bee orchid of Europe and North Africa has had to develop a flower that resembles a female bee in order to get pollinated. Male bees are attracted to it, and in their attempts to mate with the bee flower, get the sticky pollen on their heads, which then rubs off inside the next bee orchid they try to mate with.

Because they are so beautiful and showy, orchids have become very popular as houseplants. A large international industry now supports the raising and distribution of orchids.

The Barbary sheep, also known as the aoudad, is well adapted to the maquis and garrigue, able to expertly climb the steep slopes and survive without water.

Animals

The dense, low shrub growth of the matorral provides many nesting sites, good cover, and ample food for many animal species. Insects are particularly diverse, and most of the insect species of Europe are present in the Mediterranean Basin.

Mammals that use the maquis and garrigue include red fox, common jackal, wild boar, Barbary sheep, and many species of rodents. Bird species are very diverse, including a number of endemic species. Because of the high number of rodent in these communities, many raptors commonly hunt the matorral. These include the golden eagle, the short-toed eagle, the booted eagle, and the lesser kestrel. Reptile diversity is also high in the Mediterranean shrublands.

Human History

Many of the lands surrounding the Mediterranean Sea have been settled by humans for over 1,000 years. Prior to this, the area was covered with a mostly unbroken carpet of evergreen trees and shrubs. Agriculture began to impact soil and vegetation as early as 2500 BCE Many forested areas were the first to go, as wood was needed for building and heating. The land also needed to be cleared for farming and pastureland. Many different types of crops were grown in the valleys, while fruit and nut trees did very well on the hillsides.

The success of agriculture in the region was made profitable by the ease of transport of trading materials on ships traveling the relatively calm Mediterranean Sea. This economic development was one of the major reasons for the rise of Greek and Roman civilization.

The erosion caused by forest clearing and the damage to the vegetation by domesticated goats caused flooding, drying up of springs, and small-scale climate change. All the soils that washed down from the hillsides collected along the coasts of the Mediterranean Sea, creating marshes and swamps. As a result, the mosquito-borne disease malaria became a huge problem. All these consequences of the environmental changes may have contributed to the decline of the powerful Greek and Roman civilizations.

As populations declined due to disease, many farms were abandoned. Once the eroded hillsides eventually stabilized, maquis and garrigue naturally became established on the dry soils. These formations eventually succeeded to other vegetation types, including forest and grassland.

If left alone, maquis may become "stuck" in a state of poor diversity for centuries. For example, hundreds of acres in Spain are covered with a dwarf form of kermes oak. However, in most cases, shepherding and infrequent natural fires are maintaining this expression of the scrub biome.

CONCLUSION

A DELICATE BALANCE

Many natural ecosystems can clearly be seen as existing outside of the world of humans: wide expanses of the Arctic tundra; high peaks in the Tien Shan Mountains of Asia; the shifting sands of the Patagonian deserts; or the deep, dark boreal forests of Canada. Scientists study the various species, processes, and interactions that make up all of these individual systems and even the connections between each of them as related to climate and geology. This information can help government bodies, nonprofit groups, and individuals work to save large wilderness areas or a small urban park from being developed or changed.

This effort to protect wild areas often pits environmentalists against developers or others who want to utilize the natural resources found in these areas—oil, water, trees—to provide for the needs of the rapidly growing human population. However, viewing nature as separate from the man-made world makes people think in an us-versus-them way.

If ever there were a biome to confuse this seemingly clear-cut debate, it's the mediterranean scrub. Most of these formations have had such a long relationship with human culture that it is impossible to separate the natural from the human-influenced.

*The beauty of the maquis, seen here in springtime, has attracted people for ages.
These and other formations of mediterranean scrub are important both ecologically
and historically, evolving with humans for centuries.*

The Mediterranean Basin in particular, with its long history of human use, has been evolving within a matrix of agriculture, grazing lands, rural settlements, and even cities for thousands of years. It is difficult to determine what the "original" vegetation there might have been.

The Chilean matorral is most likely a product of human interaction with the environment. Most of the plants that grow in the matorral exist in shrub form in an open landscape because of all the cultivation, grazing, and burning that Incans and Spaniards have practiced over hundreds of years.

So many species of plants and animals have been exchanged between the different formations that any attempt at ecological restoration would be a monumental if not impossible, task. Australia has been trying to eradicate the European rabbit from most of the country for more than one hundred years, for example.

This interaction between humans and the environment—their joint evolution—brings into question the whole idea of a "natural" ecosystem. What is natural? What is man-made? *Can* we bring the natural ecosystems back? *Should* we?

As we see so many forests, grasslands, shrublands, and species of plants and animals disappear as humans continue to provide for a growing population, these questions become more and more important. There is hardly a spot on Earth that hasn't been influenced by humans in some way.

However, perhaps the debate shouldn't be centered on how much of the land *we* need to provide us with more clothes, more power, more things, but rather how much *other species* need to simply survive. Looking outside ourselves may be the best way to keep the planet diverse, thriving, and providing for our needs for a long time to come.

GLOSSARY

adaptation—A change in physical appearance or behavior that improves an organism's ability to interact with its environment.

annual—A plant that sprouts from a seed, grows, reproduces, and dies within the span of one year.

biogeography—The study of the distribution of living things; what grows or lives where.

carnivore—An animal that eats mostly meat.

climax—The stage of development in a plant community in which the community is able to maintain itself without changing to another level of succession.

diversity—Variety; when referring to living things or ecosystems, the term biodiversity is often used.

dormancy—A stage in the life cycle of plants or animals in which their life processes become suspended in response to adverse environmental conditions or a change to another developmental stage. In scrub communities, many plants become dormant during the dry summers.

ecological restoration—Bringing a community of plants and animals back to an area where they had been removed or destroyed. This can involve the replanting and reintroduction of species and restoration of natural flows to rivers that had been channeled or dammed.

ecologists—Scientists who study the relationships between organisms and their environments.

endangered—A designation indicating that a bird, plant, or other organism is in danger of extinction.

endemic—Native to and existing only in a particular location, such as an island or a mountain range.

estivate—A form of dormancy in animals that occurs during the summer. Frogs burrow into the mud and estivate in regions that become dry for the summer.

evolution—The long-term process whereby an organism or species physically adapts to changing environmental conditions.

glacial period—A time of colder climate in geological history, when immense ice sheets extended well south from the poles, covering a large amount of the continents.

heathlands—A shrubland growing on acidic soils, characterized by ericaceous plants. The most common of these is heather, for which the shrubland is named. Many of these communities are unintentionally created and maintained by humans.

herbivore—An animal that eats mostly plants.

lignotubers—The woody, thick burl that forms at the base of some plants. It stores food for the plant and holds buds from which sprouts grow. When a scrub plant is top-killed by fire, new growth arises from the buds in the lignotubers.

magma—Molten rock beneath Earth's crust.

microclimate—The climate of a small area—for example, a small valley or exposed ridgetop.

mosaic—A patchwork of plant communities growing within a region.

Pangaea—The supercontinent from which all six of Earth's continents formed in a process that began about 250 million years ago.

perennial—A plant that can survive for three or more years, relying on underground root reserves.

photosynthesis—The process whereby plants absorb water and carbon dioxide and, using energy from the sun, convert them into carbohydrates (sugars) needed for plant growth.

raptor—A large, predatory, carnivorous bird, such as a hawk, falcon, eagle, or owl; a bird of prey.

rhizome—The underground stem of a plant from which shoots grow.

sedimentary—Rock formed from deposition of sand, silt, or clay, often in a water environment. The sediment becomes compressed and, after million of years under pressure, is transformed into rock.

species—The finest level of classification of living things. It identifies a particular organism, such as a pocket gopher.

succession—The natural course of development of plant communities from the colonization of bare ground through the self-maintaining climax stage.

tectonic plate—The pieces of the lithosphere, Earth's crust, that ride above the molten mantle. Continental plates are as much as 155 miles (250 km) thick, while oceanic plates can be 62 miles (100 km) thick.

understory—The ground layer of a forest, woodland, or shrubland, usually including herbaceous plants and grasses.

watershed—The area of land that drains into a river system.

FIND OUT MORE

Books

De Medeiros, Michael. *Chaparral.* New York: Weigl Publishers, 2006.

Quinn, Ronald D. *Introduction to California Chaparral.* Berkeley, CA: University of California Press, 2006.

Tocci, Salvatore. *The Chaparral: Life on the Scrubby Coast.* New York: Franklin Watts, 2004.

Whitfield, Philip. *Biomes and Habitats.* New York: Macmillan Reference USA, 2002.

Web Sites

http://www.lalc.k12.ca.us/target/units/chaparral
Chaparral: A Forgotten Habitat Resource Unit includes information about California chaparral and a virtual tour of a state park.

http://www.specialspecies.com/Pages/kid_creations/chaparral/chaparral.html
Good information about plants of the chaparral.

http://www.blueplanetbiomes.org/chaparral.htm
This site provides basic information about chaparral and other scrub formations.

http://www.nceas.ucsb.edu/nceas-web/kids/biomes/biomes_home.htm
The Kids Do Ecology page of the National Center for Ecological Analysis and
Synthesis has concise information on the world's biomes and links to other
Web sites.

http://www.cnps.org/programs/education/chaparral.htm
The kids' page of the California Native Plant Society, featuring information on
chaparral and fire.

BIBLIOGRAPHY

Age Co., Ltd., The. "Reclaiming our enchanted forest" http://www.theage.com.au/
August 4, 2004.

Arroyo, Mary T. Kalin, Paul H. Zedler, Marilyn D. Fox, eds. *Ecology and Biogeography of
Mediterranean Ecosystems in Chile, California, and Australia.*
New York: Springer-Verlag. 1995.

Barbour, Michael G., and William Dwight Billings, eds. *North American Terrestrial
Vegetation.* Cambridge, UK: Cambridge University Press, 2000.

Barbour, Michael G., Jack H. Burk, and Wanna D. Pitts. *Terrestrial Plant Ecology.* Menlo
Park, CA: Benjamin/Cummings Publishing Co., Inc. 1980.

Bendix, Jacob. "Pre-European Fire in California Chaparral." In *Fire, Native Peoples, and
the Natural Landscape* Thomas R. Vale, ed. Washington, D.C.: Island Press. 2002.

Bird Life International. "Birds Australia." http://www.birdsaustralia.com.au. 1995-2004.

Blondel, Jacques and James Aronson. *Biology and Wildlife of the Mediterranean Region* Oxford, UK: Oxford University Press. 1999.

Bolen, Eric G. *Ecology of North America.* New York: John Wiley and Sons, Inc. 1998.

Cape Nature Conservation. http://www.capenature.org.za. 2004.

Cody, Martin L. "Diversity, Rarity, and Conservation in Mediterranean-Climate Regions." In *Conservation Biology: The Science and Scarcity of Diversity,* Michael E. Soule, ed. Sunderland, MA: Sinauer Assoc., Inc. Publishers. 1986.

diCastri, Francesco, David W. Goodall, and Raymond L. Specht, eds. *Ecosystems of the World 11: Mediterranean-Type Shrublands.* Amsterdam, the Netherlands: Elsevier Scientific Publishing Co. 1981.

Gleason, Henry A. and Arthur Cronquist. *The Natural Geography of Plants.* New York: Columbia University Press. 1964.

Grove, A. T. and Oliver Rackham. *The Nature of Mediterranean Europe: An Ecological History.* New Haven, CT: Yale University Press. 2001.

International Marketing Council of South Africa. http://www.safrica.info. 2004.

Kricher, John C., and Gordon Morrison. *A Field Guide to the Ecology of Western Forests.* Boston, MA: Houghton Mifflin Co. 1993.

Mc Neil, J. P. *The Mountains of the Mediterranean World: An Environmental History.* Cambridge, UK: Cambridge University Press. 1992.

Rebelo, Tony. "Fynbos Biome." Vegetation of South Africa, Lesotho, and Swaziland.

Rodrigue, Christine M. "Biomes Dominated by Shrubs." http://www.csulb.edu/~rodrigue/geog140/lectures/shrubbiomes.html: California State University, Long Beach. 2001.

Stein, Bruce A., Lynn S. Kutner, and Jonathan S. Adams. *Precious Heritage: The Status of Biodiversity in the United States.* Oxford, UK: Oxford University Press. 2000.

Stern, Kingsley R. *Introductory Plant Biology, edition seven.* Dubuque, IA: Wm. C. Brown Publishers. 1997.

Woodward, Susan L. "Introduction to Biomes." http://www.runet.edu/~swoodwar/CLASSES/GEOG235/biomes/intro.html : Radford University Geography Department, 1996.

World Wildlife Fund. "Mediterranean Forests, Woodlands, and Scrub." http://www.worldwildlife.org/wildworld. 2001.

Page numbers in **boldface** are illustrations.

Tom Warhol is a photographer, writer, and naturalist from Massachusetts, where he lives with his wife, their dog, and two cats. He holds both a BFA in photography and an MS in forest ecology. Tom Warhol has worked for conservation groups such as The Nature Conservancy, managing nature preserves, and The American Chestnut Foundation, helping to grow blight-resistant American chestnut trees. He currently works for the Massachusetts Riverways Program, helping to care for sick, injured, and resident hawks, eagles, and owls. In addition to the Earth's Biomes series, Warhol has authored books for Marshall Cavendish Benchmark's AnimalWays series, including *Hawks* and *Eagles*. He also writes for newspapers such as the *Boston Globe*. His landscape, nature, and wildlife photographs can be seen in exhibitions, in publications, and on his Web site, www.tomwarhol.com.